D1397943

TRICERATOPS

by Janet Riehecky
illustrated by Diana Magnuson

THE CHILD'S WORLD

MANKATO, MN

Grateful appreciation is expressed to Bret S. Beall,
Curatorial Coordinator for the Department of Geology,
Field Museum of Natural History, Chicago, Illinois,
who reviewed this book to insure its accuracy.

Library of Congress Cataloging in Publication Data

Riehecky, Janet, 1953-
    Triceratops / by Janet Riehecky ; illustrated by Diana L.
Magnuson.
    p. cm. — (Dinosaurs)
    Summary: An introduction to what is known and hypothesized about
the dinosaur triceratops, which means three-horned face.
    ISBN 0-89565-422-9
    1. Triceratops—Juvenile literature.   [1. Triceratops.
2. Dinosaurs.]   I. Magnuson, Diana, ill.   II. Title.   III. Series:
Riehecky, Janet, 1953-   Dinosaurs.
QE862.D5R44   1988
567.9'7—dc19   88-508
                                                                      CIP
                                                                       AC

© 1988 The Child's World
Mankato, MN
All rights reserved. Printed in U.S.A.

TRICERATOPS

Dinosaurs lived on the earth a long time ago.

Some people think that they weren't very smart. But when it came to survival, dinosaurs knew how to use their heads.

For instance, there were dinosaurs that needed to eat a lot. They had jaws that were hinged so their mouths could open very wide for BIG mouthfuls.

Other dinosaurs needed to be able to escape into deep water to survive. These dinosaurs had noses on top of their heads, so they could go into very deep water and still breathe.

One type of dinosaur had a skull with ten inches of solid bone on top. It could crash headfirst into anything and not even get a headache.

Still another had a showy crest on top
of its head. That helped it get attention
from dinosaurs of the opposite sex.

But there was one type of dinosaur who really had a head for solving problems—a huge head. This dinosaur's head was six feet long, almost one-third of its whole body. It had a thick collar for protection and three sharp horns for fighting. This dinosaur was the Triceratops (try-SER-a-tops). Its name means "three-horned face."

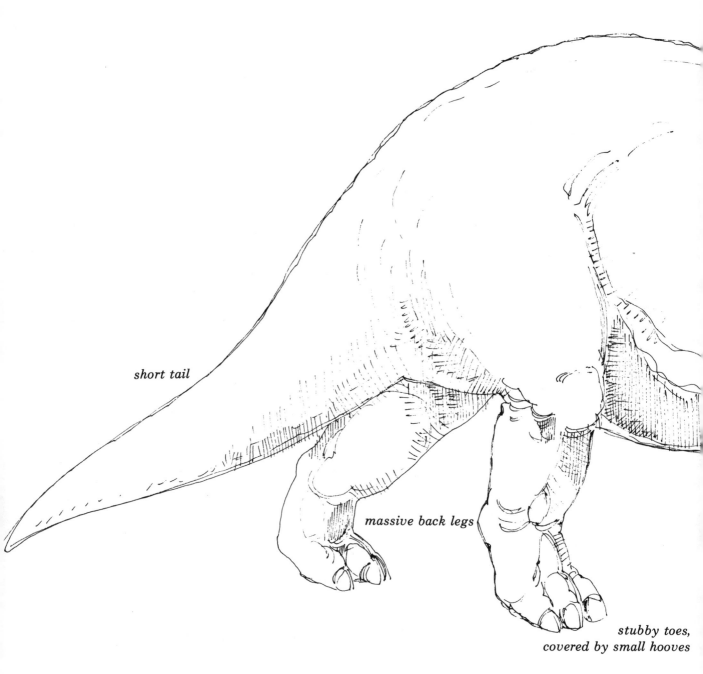

short tail

massive back legs

stubby toes,
covered by small hooves

The Triceratops was just an average-sized dinosaur—which meant it was about the size of a pick-up truck! It grew about ten feet tall, twenty-five feet long, and weighed about eight tons.

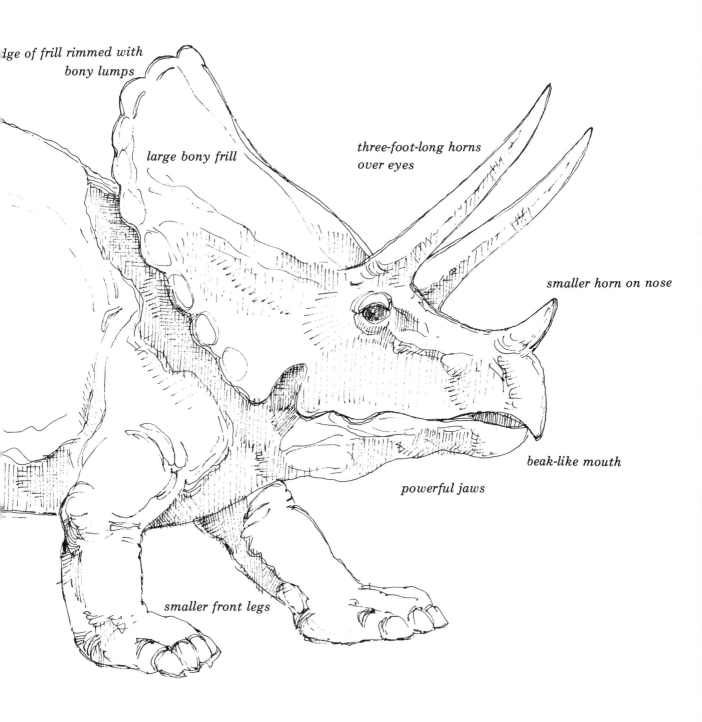

lge of frill rimmed with
bony lumps

large bony frill

three-foot-long horns
over eyes

smaller horn on nose

beak-like mouth

powerful jaws

smaller front legs

Triceratops was a plant-eating dinosaur, but it was the most dangerous plant eater ever to live. Even the mighty Tyrannosaurus must have thought twice before attacking it.

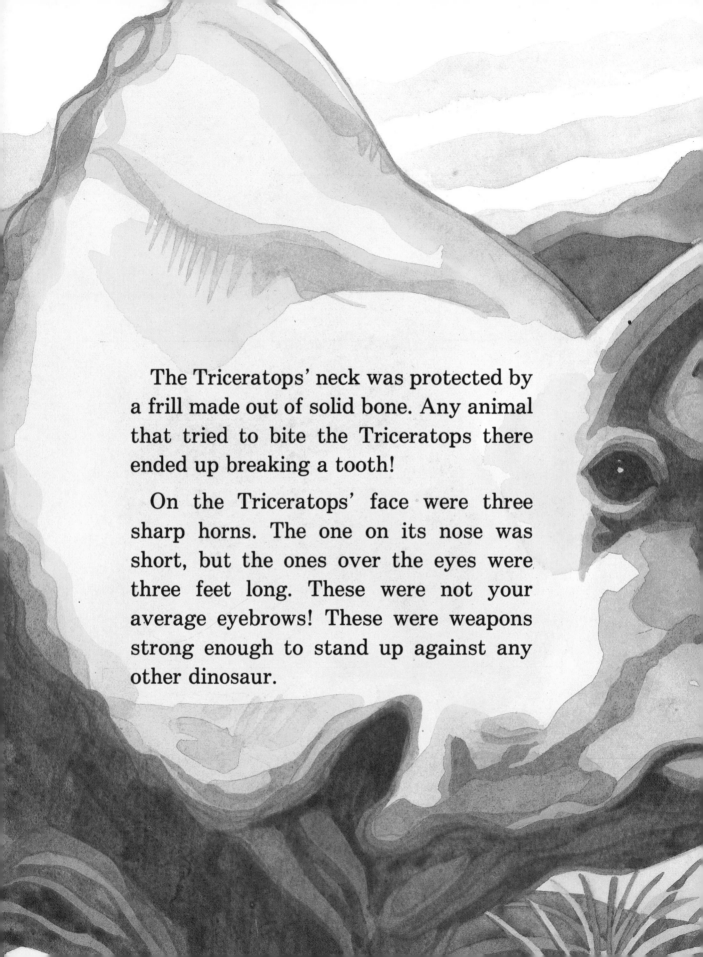

The Triceratops' neck was protected by a frill made out of solid bone. Any animal that tried to bite the Triceratops there ended up breaking a tooth!

On the Triceratops' face were three sharp horns. The one on its nose was short, but the ones over the eyes were three feet long. These were not your average eyebrows! These were weapons strong enough to stand up against any other dinosaur.

Even the mouth of the Triceratops could help it fight. The Triceratops didn't have any teeth in the front of its mouth, but it did have a sharp beak, like a parrot's beak. In its cheeks it had sharp teeth that went together like scissor blades. The teeth were stacked four deep in its jaws, so if one came out, it would be replaced by the one just under it.

The Triceratops didn't go around starting fights, but if somebody else started one, it was ready.

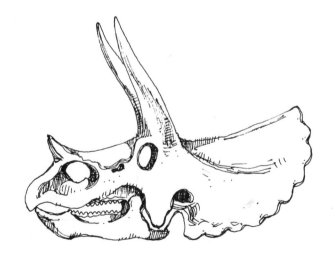

The Triceratops lived in high, dry groves. It ate ferns, cycads, and palm leaves. Its beak and sharp teeth were good at slicing through tough plants.

The Triceratops traveled in small herds
as many other dinosaurs did. The herds
roamed the uplands, looking for food and
minding their own business. They weren't
looking for trouble, but sometimes trouble found them.

Sometimes another dinosaur would attack a herd of Triceratops. Then the Triceratops used their heads.

Scientists think they formed a circle around the smaller, weaker Triceratops. Then the larger, stronger ones would face out, challenging the attacker with their horns. Working together like this, they could probably defeat even the terrible Tyrannosaurus.

The horns of the Triceratops were such good weapons that the Triceratops found another use for them—fighting each other. They didn't know how to vote for a leader of a herd, so scientists think they fought to see who got to be the leader, just as many animals with horns do today.

The fight might have gone like this: two Triceratops would lock horns. Then they would push and twist each other in something like a wrestling contest. The winner would get to be the boss.

Scientists don't know much about the family life of Triceratops. They have found nests of eggs from Protoceratops, an ancester of Triceratops, so they think Triceratops probably laid eggs too.

Scientists also think this dinosaur may have taken care of its babies after they were born, instead of just leaving them on their own as many reptiles do. But we don't know this for sure.

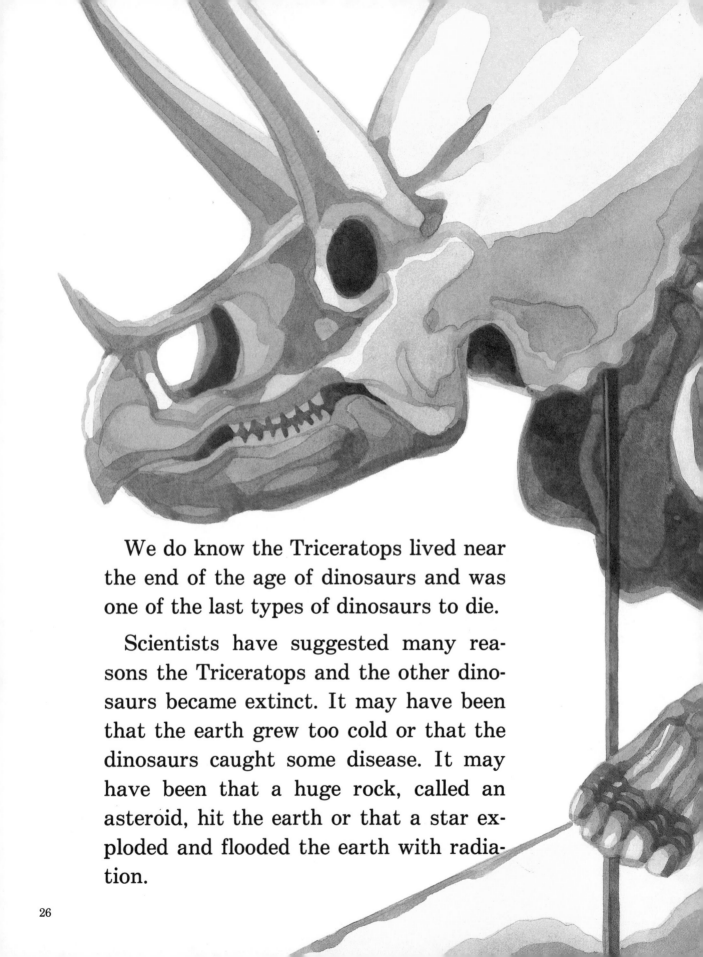

We do know the Triceratops lived near the end of the age of dinosaurs and was one of the last types of dinosaurs to die.

Scientists have suggested many reasons the Triceratops and the other dinosaurs became extinct. It may have been that the earth grew too cold or that the dinosaurs caught some disease. It may have been that a huge rock, called an asteroid, hit the earth or that a star exploded and flooded the earth with radiation.

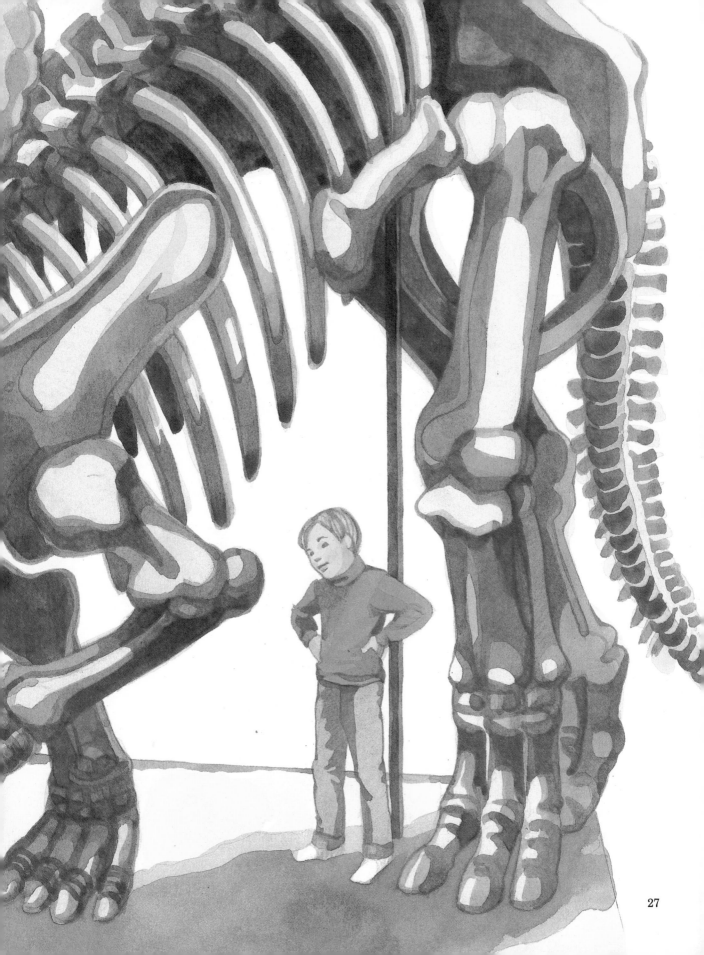

Whatever caused the extinction may never be known.

But dinosaurs left behind teeth, bones,
and mummies.

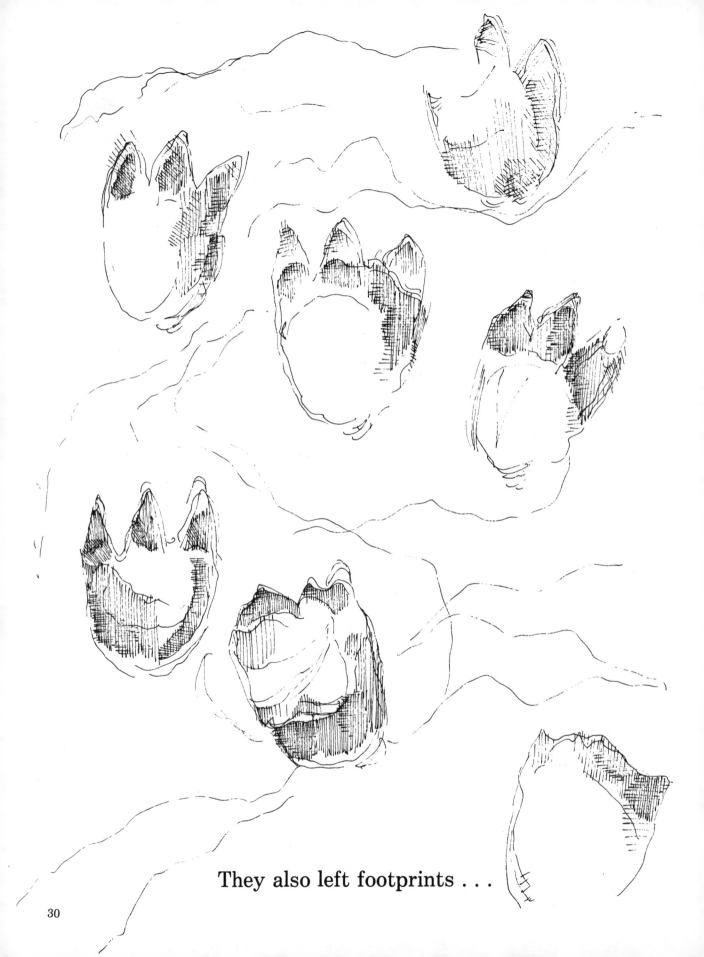

They also left footprints . . .

and eggs.

From these things we can learn much about those fascinating dinosaurs.

 **Dinosaur Fun**

Scientists can learn a lot about a dinosaur by the footprints it leaves behind. You can make "dinosaur tracks" of your own! You will need:

— a large sheet of paper

— a pen

— a large potato

— a paring knife

— tempera paint

1. Cut the potato in half. Dry the cut part with a towel.

2. Draw a dinosaur footprint on the cut part of the potato with a pen. You can follow the picture on page 30.

3. With help from an adult, cut away the potato around the footprint outline. Cut away about ¼ inch.

4. Now make tracks by dipping the potato into the paint and then pressing it on the paper. You can also make another kind of dinosaur's footprint with the other half of the potato. See if you can make your tracks tell a story!